INDUSTRIAL ADOPTION OF SOLAR AIR CONDITIONING: MEASUREMENT PROBLEMS, SOLUTIONS AND MARKETING IMPLICATIONS

Jean-Marie Choffray

and

Gary L. Lilien

WP 894-76 December 1976

Abstract

Industrial adoption of capital goods typically involves several individuals with different backgrounds and job responsibilities. These individuals differ in the way they perceive and evaluate available product alternatives The measurement and consideration of these differences can lead to substantial improvements in the development of marketing strategies for new industrial products.

This paper analyzes the introduction of solar powered air conditioning aimed at the industrial market. Individuals most likely to be involved in the adoption process are identified and differences in their perceptions and evaluation criteria are measured. The investigation of these problems leads to new measurement methods and to some new tests for determining the equality of evaluation spaces. Implications for the development of a marketing plan for industrial solar air conditioning are discussed. The potential for application of the new methodology to development of marketing programs for other industrial products is also reviewed.

A significant difference between individual and organizational adoption of energy alternatives (or, in fact, products of any sort) is that organizations typically have several individuals involved in the adoption process. These individuals differ in both their perceptions of available product alternatives and their evaluation criteria. Specific consideration of these differences in a product development procedure leads to improvements in product positioning and opens new marketing strategy alternatives. This paper suggests how differences in product perception and evaluation criteria can be measured and how those measurements be used to improve market entry strategy for solar powered, industrial air conditioning systems.

1. Solar Energy Alternatives

Currently, over 25% of the energy used in the U.S. is consumed by heating and cooling of buildings and by providing hot water (Westinghouse phase 0 report [31]). At a conversion efficiency of 10%, 11,000 square miles of solar collectors (or 0.3% of U S. land area) could have satisfied the 1970 water and space heating and cooling needs of the U.S. (Williams [33]). In light of increasing costs and diminishing supplies of fossil fuels as well as our professed need for energy independence, solar energy is an alternative to be considered

A recent study compared the cost of conventional and solar space heating, amortizing the solar system capital cost over 20 years at 6% interest, and found that even at $\$2/ft^2$ for solar collectors (an optimistically low price) there are few U.S. areas where such systems are cost effective cur-

to be in water heating. About 4% of the U.S. energy consumption goes for water heating. (Westinghouse phase 0 report [31]). Water heating is also a simple and effective application of solar technology and there is much literature regarding its feasibility and efficiency (Daniels [8]). In fact, there are over 2.5 million solar water heaters now in use in Japan and over 100,000 in Israel (Williams [33]).

Solar water heating systems have not been adopted in the U.S. in any major way even in the South or Southwest; there are now about 8,000 such systems currently in use in the southern U.S. (New England Electric System [23]). Why aren't there more? Certainly there are key economic and financial considerations hindering adoption of these systems: they cost the consumer more now, although they promise future savings. A significant amount of research has centered around constraints and incentives surrounding the adoption of solar heating and cooling equipment (see Arthur D. Little [19] report, for example) Little of this research, though, focuses on non-economic factors affecting adoption. An exception is a report on the market potential for solar water heaters in New England which suggests that personal, lifestyle and system-design characteristics strongly affect consumers' propensity to adopt solar water heaters (Lilien and Johnston [18])

Although immediate prospects for an economically viable solar-powered alternative are not great, it is important to note that space cooling is the fastest growing area of U.S. energy use, projected to account for over 5% of U.S. energy demand by 1980 (Westinghouse phase 0 report [31]). The greatest portion of this demand is for use in industrial buildings Thus, a considerable amount of fossil fuel could be saved by wide scale adoption

System economics are important factors affecting industrial adoption. But, as in the case of solar water heaters, non-economic factors are important as well, Lehmann and O'Shaughnessy [16] indicate that price is not the primary determinant of supplier in most industrial purchasing situations. Non-economic factors affecting solar air conditioning adoption include:

- reliability
- sensitivity to climatic conditions
- company image
- protection against fuel rationing
- system complexity
- protection against power failures
- etc.

(see Lilien [17]).

It is entirely possible that a so-called cost effective solar air conditioning system may <u>not</u> be adopted for non-economic reasons or, conversely, that a system may be adopted that is not cost effective due to some of the non-economic considerations indicated above (Lilien [17]). A detailed understanding of these issues is an essential input to development of an effective marketing strategy.

2 Industrial Adoption of Energy Saving Alternatives

The industrial adoption process differs from the consumer adoption process in several respects. First, organizational buying decisions usually involve several people with varying preferences, and perceptions and whose responsibilities differ. Second, industrial purchasing decisions tend to involve more technical complexities related to the specific product being purchased. Third, the organizational adoption process can be separated into phases more easily than the consumer adoption process, as different individuals are usually associated with different phases. Finally, these decisions typically take longer to make, leading to lags between the application of marketing strategy and buying response (Webster and Wind [30]).

Figure 1 describes a conceptual model of the industrial adoption process for capital equipment. It is based on the assumption that the firm has recognized the need for a product from the class under study, and that the adoption decision results from a systematic decision-making process.

According to the model, environmental and organizational constraints influence the purchasing decision process by limiting the number of product alternatives of which decision participants are aware and which also satisfy organizational needs. The resulting set of feasible alternatives is the choice set of the organization, over which individual perceptions and preferences are defined. The last element of the model links individual preference to group preference through group interaction procedures. Choffray and Lilien [4] develop models of the group selection of a specific alternative from the firm's feasible set.

Choffray [5] suggests that two major sets of measurements are needed to

of the adoption decision process and those dealing with the differences in perception and evaluation criteria among participants in that process.

Questions dealing with the structure of the adoption process and the identification of clusters of organizations that exhibit similar patterns of involvement in their adoption process are dealt with elsewhere by Choffray [5] Here we treat the critical problem of how participants in the adoption process for energy saving equipment differ in the way they perceive and evaluate available alternatives.

Choffray's [5] work on microsegment analysis suggests that the potential market for industrial air conditioning systems can be segmented according to what individual responsibilities are most likely to be involved in the decision process. This information is critical to the development of sensible marketing strategies for new industrial products, especially if decision participants who exert similar responsibilities in their respective organizations do in fact differ in the way they perceive and evaluate available product alternatives. A similar concern about the differential perception of innovations by different groups of individuals involved in their adoption was also expressed by Rogers and Shoemaker [24].

The problems we investigate in the next sections, then, are:

1. How do these different groups of potential decision participants differ in the way they perceive available alternatives, including the new air conditioning system?

2. How do these groups of decision participants differ in their evaluation criteria?

3. What evaluation criteria most heavily affect product preferences for each of these different groups of individuals?

The development of methodology to systematically, consistently and accurately

FIGURE 1

A CONCEPTUAL MODEL OF THE INDUSTRIAL ADOPTION PROCESS

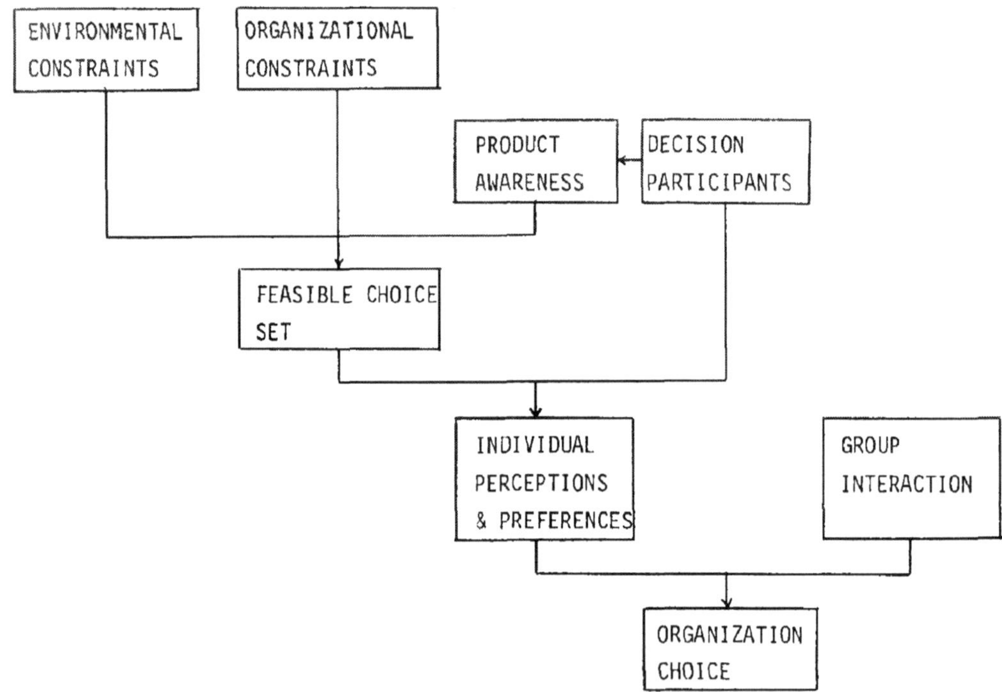

3 The Data and Measurement Procedure

The data used for this analysis were collected as part of an EDA funded study to explore the U.S. market potential for solar powered industrial air conditioning A sample of firms was selected by size, SIC code and geographic area and a senior management member was identified He was sent a personal letter asking for the names of two or three members of his organization most likely to be involved in the adoption decision process for air conditioning equipment. A detailed questionnaire was then sent to the individuals mentioned. This two-step sampling procedure was used to increase the likelihood of reaching key people in the adoption decision for this class of product.

The questionnaire requested information about the company, its requirements for products in this class, its decision process and personal information. Each respondent was also exposed to three product concept statements, accurately describing the solar alternative and two conventional cooling systems. Ratings were obtained for each of these concepts on a set of perceptual scales representing relevant attributes along which decision participants assess products in this class. Seven-point Likert scales were used for this purpose. Conditional preferences for the alternatives (see Wildt and Bruno [32]) were then obtained, using both rank and constant sum methods.

A similar document was prepared and sent, via the same mail-out procedure, to HVAC (Heating, Ventilating and Air Conditioning) consulting firms. The descriptions of the products (concept statements) were identical However, because certain issues are perceived differently and are of differential importance to outside versus inside company people, a slightly different set of attribute ratings was obtained from the consultants. Table 1 lists the scales

that are common to both groups and which were found relevant for this analysis.

The use of product descriptions or concept statements in marketing research is a widely accepted practice. Urban [29] and Hauser and Urban [13] use such concept statements to assess response to changes in the design of frequently purchased consumer products. In industrial marketing, Scott and Wright [25] recently used a similar approach to investigate the organizational buyer's product evaluation process. The approach is particularly suitable in industrial marketing as the technical complexity of product alternatives and the technical orientation of decision participants make accurate product descriptions a meaningful basis for judgement. In addition, an actual physical product is generally not available in the early stage of development of new industrial products when exploratory market research is performed.

TABLE 1 ATTRIBUTES USED FOR AIR CONDITIONING SYSTEM EVALUATION

1. The system provides reliable air conditioning.
2. Adoption of the system protects against power failures.
3. The system is made up of field-proven components.
4. The system conveys the image of a modern, innovative company.
5. The system cost is acceptably low.
6. The system protects against fuel rationing.
7. The system allows us to do our part in reducing pollution.
8. System components produced by several manufacturers can be substituted for one another.
9. The system uses too many concepts that have not been fully tested.
10. The system leads to considerable energy savings.
11. The system is too complex.
12. The system provides low cost a/c.
13. The system offers a state-of-the-art solution to a/c needs.
14. The system increases the noise level in the plant.

4. Grouping of Decision Participants

In this study, likely purchase decision participants were grouped on the basis of job responsibility. This decision is consistent with Sheth's [26] contention that product perceptions and evaluation criteria tend to differ among decision participants as a result of differences in educational background, experience, sources of information, and reference groups. The existence of company policies that reward individuals for their specialized skills and viewpoints also tend to reinforce these psychological differences.

As some variation must be expected across companies in the responsibility corresponding to different job titles, a specific request was made in the questionnaire that the respondent describe his main job responsibility. Five groups of respondents were then created and are used in this analysis. We distinguish Production Engineers (PE), Corporate Engineers (CE), Plant Managers (PM), Top Managers (TM) and HVAC consultants (HC).

5.0 Product Perception Analysis

Each of the respondents was exposed to a concept statement describing (1) an absorption a/c system (ABSAIR), (2) a compression a/c system (COMAIR) and (3) the solar-powered absorption a/c system (SOLABS). (See Lilien [17] for a technical description of these various a/c systems). Our task here is to determine if and how the groups of decision participants -- PE, CE, PM, TM, HC -- differ in the way they perceive these three product alternatives.

5.1 Perceptual Analysis Methodology

Figure 2 outlines the methodology developed for this purpose. For each group of participants, concept ratings are obtained (A). Within each group, concept ambiguity is tested via one-way multivariate analysis of variance (B). Assuming that the concept statements have been carefully developed and present an accurate description of each available alternative, the existence of ambiguity of concept perception warns the researcher to be careful in his interpretation of the preference data Methodologies developed so far in the consumer goods area have usually overlooked this problem.

For each concept statement, a multivariate profile analysis is then performed (C), to investigate the existence of perceptual differences among the five groups of decision participants. Tests for profile parallelism (D) and for equality of levels (E) are applied. (See Figure 3 for an illustration of the concept of profile parallelism and profile level equality) The hypothesis of profile parallelism is tested by the largest characteristic root criterion using the Heck statistic (see Morrison [22]). The hypothesis of

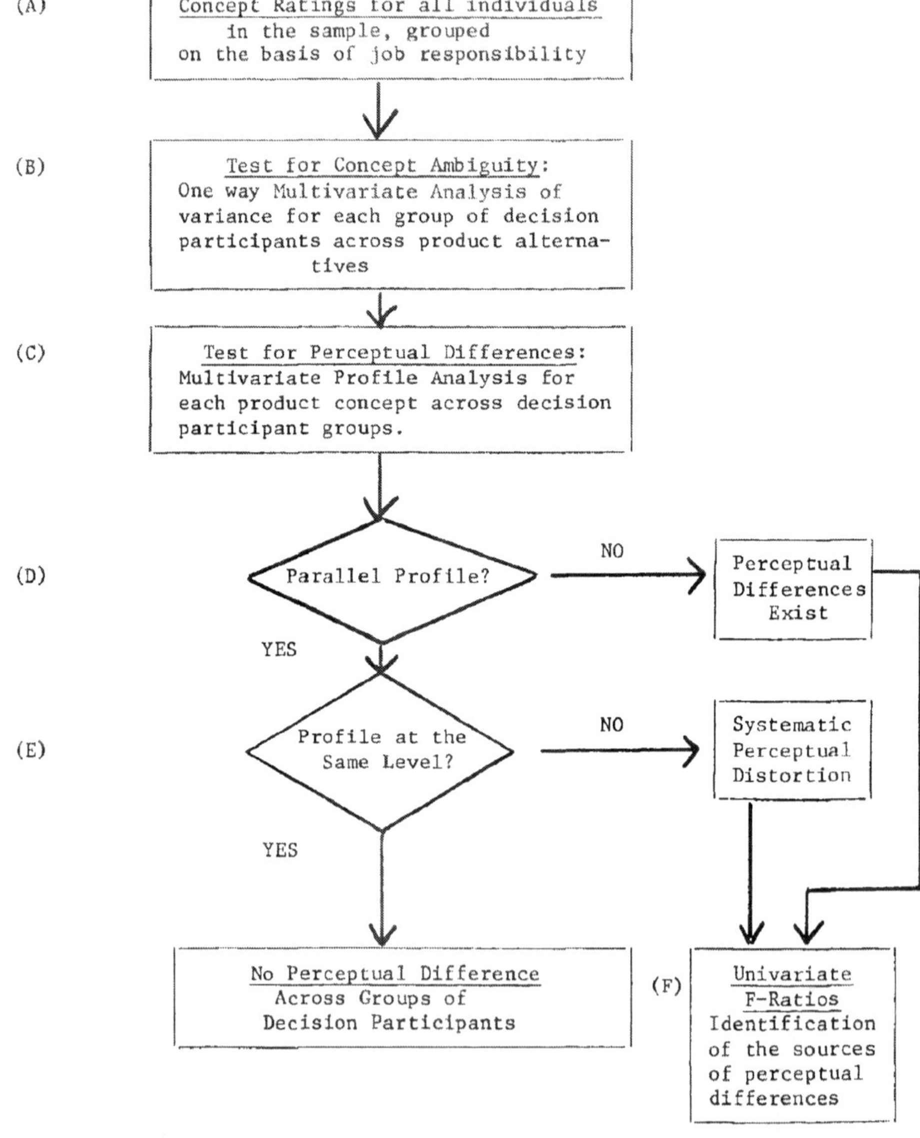
(A)
Concept Ratings for all individuals
in the sample, grouped
on the basis of job responsibility
(B)
Test for Concept Ambiguity:
One way Multivariate Analysis of
variance for each group of decision
participants across product alterna-
tives
(C)
Test for Perceptual Differences:
Multivariate Profile Analysis for
each product concept across decision
participant groups.
(D)
Parallel Profile?
NO
Perceptual
Differences
Exist
YES
(E)
Profile at the
Same Level?
NO
Systematic
Perceptual
Distortion
YES
No Perceptual Difference
Across Groups of
Decision Participants
(F)
Univariate
F-Ratios
Identification
of the sources
of perceptual
differences

variance on the sums of the responses of each individual across the 5 groups. If the groups do differ in their perceptions, univariate F-ratios (F) are obtained to isolate those basic attributes that are the major sources of the perceptual difference.

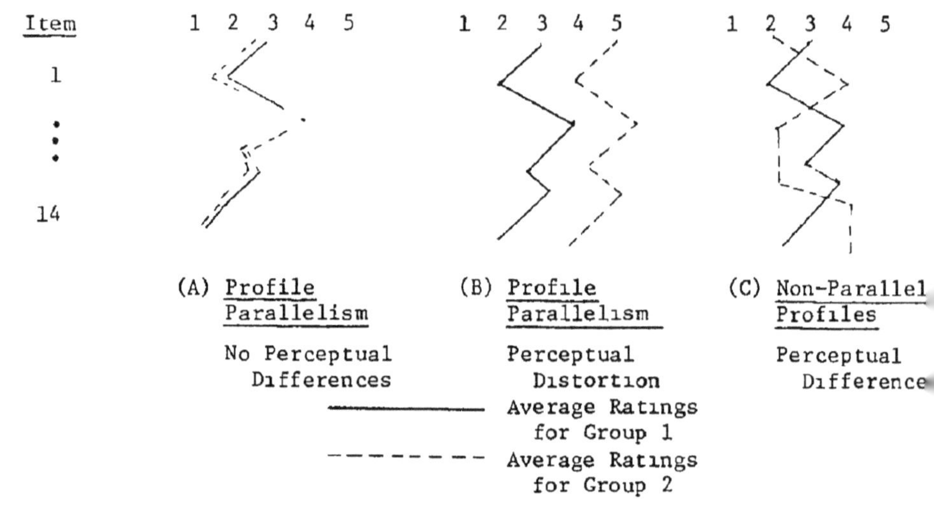

FIGURE 3

THE CONCEPT OF PERCEPTUAL EQUIVALENCE

5.2 Perceptual Analysis Results

Application of step B of the methodology led to the conclusion that each group of likely decision participants perceived the three available alternatives as substantially different (see Choffray [5]). This result was not unexpected as the three products indeed presented important differences.

Table 2 gives the major statistical results for the multivariate profile analysis. Significant differences are registered between groups of decision participants in the way they perceive each product concept. This is seen through the strong statistical significance of the Heck Criteria.

Analysis of the differences (F) via one-way univariate analysis of variance, suggests that all attributes retained in this analysis contribute to perceptual differences among at least two groups of decision participants. Table 3 presents these univariate F-ratios for PM and HC. Plant managers (PM) view solar air conditioning (SOLABS) as a more substantial means of protection against power failures. They also tend to consider it as more cost effective than HVAC consultants do. Finally, plant managers view SOLABS as a complex system whose components have not been fully tested, but which provide a state-of-the-art solution to industrial air conditioning needs. HVAC consultants' perception of SOLABS differ considerably in this last respect

In summary, the results of this part of the analysis confirm the existence of substantial perceptual differences among the different groups of decision participants. And the selection of the scales seemed appropriate as they all contributed to the differences noted among groups of decision participants.

TABLE 2· MULTIVARIATE PROFILE ANALYSIS RESULTS

Product Concept	Heck Criterion For Profile Parallelism
COMAIR	.646 * (s=4.m=4.m=98.5)
ABSAIR	.260 * (s=4,m=4,n=94.5)
SOLABS	.347 * (s=4,m=4,n=97)

* Significant at the 01 level.

TABLE 3: COMPARISON OF GROUP MEANS FOR THE THREE PRODUCT CONCEPTS

PLANT MANAGERS VS. HVAC CONSULTANTS

	COMAIR			ABSAIR			SOLABS		
	PM	HC	F-RATIO (1,112)	PM	HC	F-RATIO (1,107)	PM	HC	F-RATIO (1,110)
EM 1	5.91	5.96	.05	4.81	5.47	3.97**	3.91	3.87	.02
EM 2	1.83	1.54	2.82*	2.57	2.48	.04	4.57	3.18	8.27***
EM 3	5.87	6.10	1.27	5.14	5.57	1.86	3.35	3.25	.08
EM 4	4.30	3.30	8.85***	4.05	3.03	7.28***	5.83	5.70	.15
EM 5	5.09	5.52	2.90*	3.24	3.22	.00	2.48	1.89	3.93**
EM 6	3.26	3.25	.00	2.67	2.19	1.59	5.78	5.49	.74
EM 7	3.91	3.67	.37	3.48	2.55	6.52**	6.04	5.83	.46
EM 8	4.83	5.12	.71	3.71	3.84	.08	3.61	4.17	1.80
EM 9	2.35	1.79	3.79*	2.95	2.34	2.88*	4.74	4.08	2.83*
EM 10	2.65	3.18	2.82*	3.19	2.56	2.93*	5.70	6.10	2.25
EM 11	3.04	2.12	11.78***	3.62	2.97	2.91*	3.61	3.57	.01
EM 12	3.26	4.54	18.34***	3.33	3.16	.21	4.96	4.21	3.10*
EM 13	4.35	4.64	.72	3.57	3.85	.55	5.52	4.56	6.44**
EM 14	4.96	4.82	.15	2.57	2.05	2.87*	1.83	2.08	.73

nificant at .10 level ** Significant at .05 level *** Significant at .01 level

6.0 Product Evaluation Space Analysis

Although individuals can accurately describe their perceptions of product alternatives on a set of perceptual scales, it is unlikely that they consider all these attributes independently in a choice situation (see Miller [20]). Several basic attrinutes of the product class under investigation may be interrelated because they comprise the same underlying evaluation criteria (Howard and Sheth [14]).

In this part of the analysis, we are concerned with the evaluation criteria that each group of potential decision participants uses assuming that all individuals within a given group use the same evaluation criteria. An individual's evaluation of a product alternative may then be seen as a vector or coordinates in this reduced product evaluation space (Howard and Sheth [14], Allaire [1], Hauser [12]).

Two questions arise immediately:

- Is the dimensionality of the evaluation spaces (that is, the number of evaluation criteria) the same for the different groups of potential decision participants?
- If so, are the evaluation criteria essentially equivalent?

The methodology outlined below addresses both these issues.

6.1 Product Evaluation Space Methodology

Figure 4 outlines the steps in the evaluation space analysis. Concept ratings are obtained for each concept statements (A). Then, variance-covariance matrices are calculated for each group of decision participant across concepts (B). This approach was suggested by Urban [29] as a way to

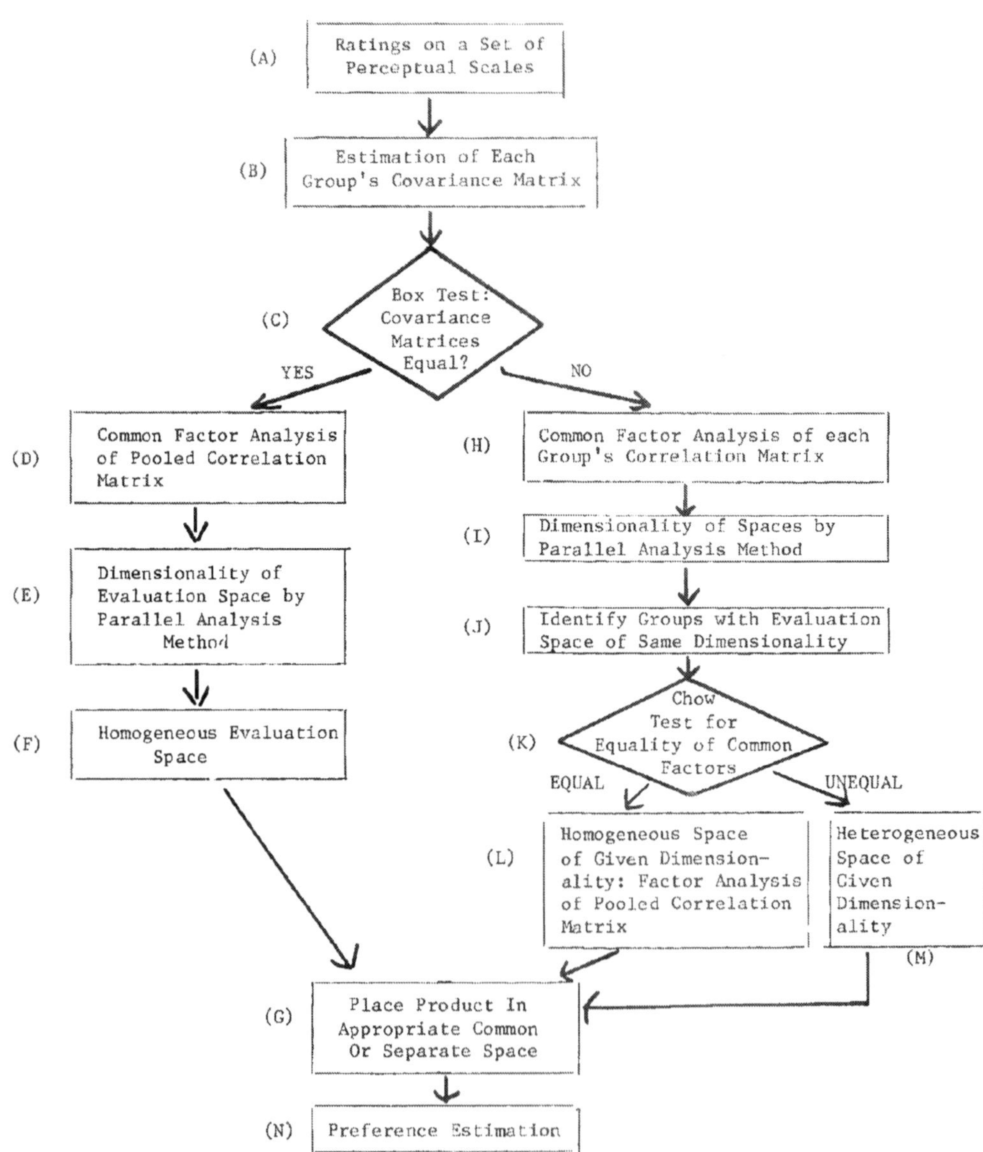

FIGURE 4: OUTLINE OF EVALUATION SPACE METHODOLOGY

space. It is intuitively appealing, as it implies that for each group all products in the product class are assessed along the same set of evaluation criteria. Box's [2] test is then used to test the equality of these variance-covariance matrices (C). If the matrices are found to be equal they are pooled, factor analyzed and product alternatives as perceived by each individual are placed in the common evaluation space (D,E,F,G).

Box's test is very powerful, however (Greenstreet and Connor [9], Cooley and Lohnes [7]). Rejection of the hypothesis of equality of groups' variance-covariance matrices should only be taken as an indicator of possible differences in the evaluation spaces of each group. Indeed, as common factor analysis does not make use of all information present in these matrices, it is possible that the evaluation spaces are similar even though the hypotheses of equality of covariance matrix is rejected.

If the hypothesis of equal variance-covariance matrices is rejected, separate factor analyses are performed for each group (H). The parallel analysis technique (Humphreys and Ilgen [15]) is then used to determine the dimensionality of the evaluation space of each group of decision participants. The method involves the factoring of a second correlation matrix identical in the number of variables and observations as the original data matrix, but obtained from randomly generated normal deviates. Recently, Montanelli and Humphreys [21] provided a method of estimating the expected values of the latent roots of random data correlation matrices with squared multiple correlations on the diagonal. This method was used here.

Inequality of dimensionality indicates the existence of a substantial difference in the evaluation space (I) Otherwise, groups of decision partici-

equality of these criteria using a modified version of Chow's test [6] (see Appendix 1 for a description of the test) (K). If the evaluation criteria are deemed similar, the concept ratings for these groups are pooled and factor analysis is performed again to determine the evaluation space common to these groups (L). For each individual, product coordinates in the appropriate evaluation space are then assessed (G).

The final step of the methodology is preference estimation (N). Once products are positioned in the appropriate evaluation space, individual preferences for the available alternatives can be linked to the products' coordinates in this space. This step of the methodology then assesses the relative importance of the evaluation criteria in the formation of preferences within decision participant groups.

6 2 Product Evaluation Space Results

Individual covariance matrices were estimated for each of the five groups (HC, PE, CE, PM and TM) using ratings obtained on the 14 perceptual scales. The Box Test was used to test the equality of these covariance matrices, giving an F-ratio of 1.80 for 408 and 226,827 degrees of freedom. The hypothesis of equal covariance matrices was then rejected and a separate principal factor analysis was performed for each group. Squared multiple correlations were used as estimates of the communalities of the original perceptual scales, and were computed within each group.

The dimensionality of each group's evaluation space was obtained by the parallel analysis method. Figure 5 presents the observed trace of eigenvalues and the zero information trace for production engineers (PE) The point at

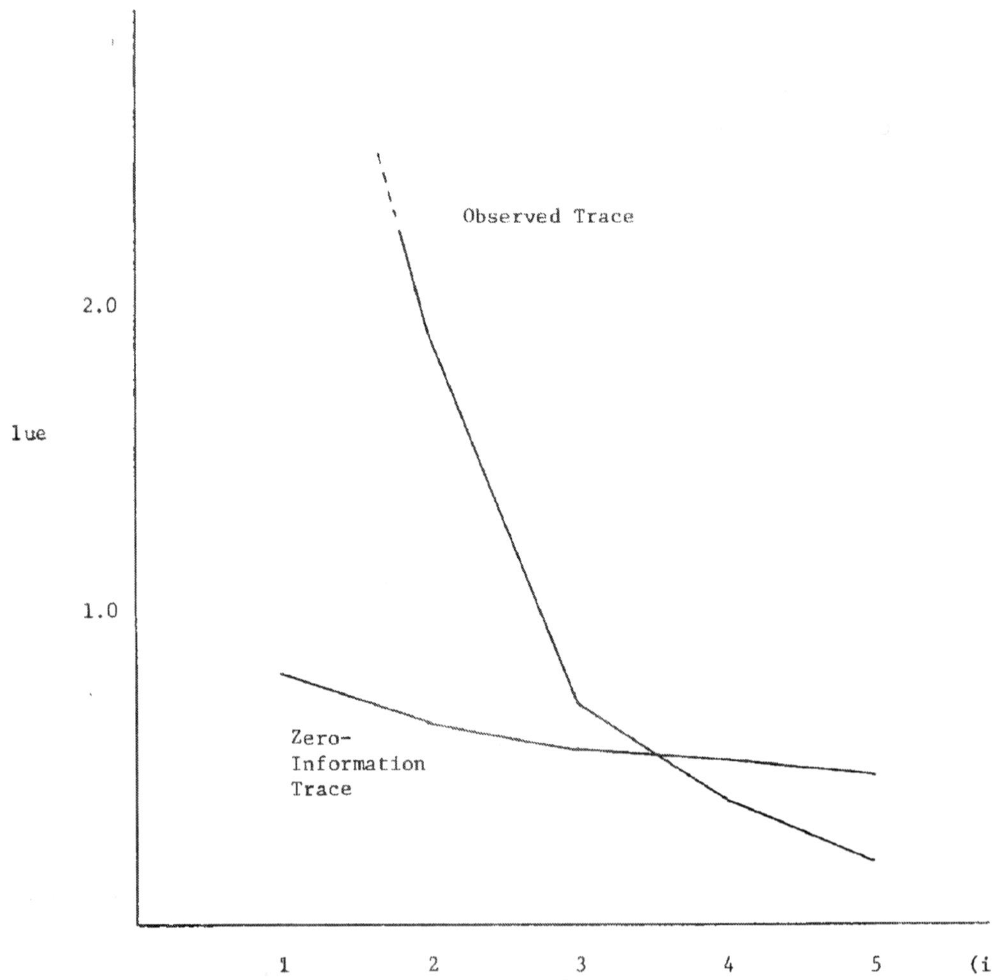

Observed Trace
2.0
lue
1.0
Zero-
Information
Trace
1
2
3
4
5
(i)
Number of Factors (i)

We are not interested in a factor that does not account for more variance than the corresponding factor obtained from distributions of random numbers. The dimensionality of the PE evaluation space is then 3. The results for the other groups are given in Table 3.

GROUP	DIMENSIONALITY OF EVALUATION SPACE
CE	2
PM	2
PE	3
TM	3
HC	3

TABLE 3: EVALUATION SPACE DIMENSIONALITY

Two groups have an evaluation space of dimensionality 2 (CE and PM) and the other three groups (PE, TM, HC) have a three-dimensional evaluation space This indicates that Production Engineers, Top Managers, and HVAC consultants who have relatively more responsibility in the decision process (see Cheston and Doucet [3]) appear to use more decision criteria. We treat the CE-PM groups first.

Separate common factor analyses were run for CE and PM and a varimax rotation was performed on each (see Appendix 2). Most similar factors were identified and their equivalence tested one at a time using a modified version of the Chow Test, as indicated in Appendix 1. Table 4 gives the results.

	F-Ratio	Degrees of Freedom	
A. Matched factors (PM_1, CE_2)	1.84	14,125	*
B. Matched factors (PM_2, CE_1)	1.48	14,125	

(Note PM_i represents the i<u>th</u> factor in the original varimax solution for PM).

* Significant at the .05 level.

TABLE 4: TEST OF FACTOR EQUALITY FOR PM AND CE

As Factor A is significantly different for the two groups (and Factor B is nearly so), we reject the hypothesis of equality of evaluation criteria for these two groups

Similarly, PE, TM and HC's have an evaluation space of dimensionality 3 Table 5 tests factor equivalence for these groups.

	F-Ratio	Degrees of Freedom	
A. Matched Factors (PE_1, TM_1, HC_1)	1.80	14,459	*
B. Matched Factors (PE_2, TM_2, HC_2)	1.91	14,459	*
C. Matched Factors (PE_3, TM_3, HC_3)	21.8	14,459	**

* Significant at .05 level

** Significant at .001 level

TABLE 5: TEST OF FACTOR EQUALITY FOR PE, TM AND HC

Thus, these groups exhibit substantial differences in their evaluation criteria and should be analyzed separately The interpretation of these evaluation criteria leads to interesting qualitative distinctions between decision participant groups. For the two factor solutions we summarize and interpret the results in Table 6

	Factor A	Factor B
Corporate Engineer (CE)	Reliability/ Field Tested First Cost Noise Level	Pollution Energy Savings/Protection Modernness
Plant Manager (PM)	Energy Savings/ Protection Modernness Low Operating Cost	Reliability/ Field Tested Modularity Noise Level

TABLE 6: COMPARISON OF FACTOR SOLUTIONS FOR CE, PM

The issue of air condition systems' initial costs does not appear to be vital to Plant Managers; modernness, energy savings and protection against fuel rationing and power failures are primary On the other hand, corporate engineers see the system's reliability and first costs as the primary issues

Similarly, Table 7 presents an interpretation of the factor solutions for the other three groups, TM, PE and HC. The composition of the first factor indicates minor differences between these groups in terms of their first evaluation criteria (TM include protection against power failures and HC do not place the same emphasis on low operating cost). Major differences, however, arise in the second and third factors. Production Engineers (PE) emphasize system complexity and modularity more than other groups First cost comes out clearly as an important element in top managers' (TM) evaluation of industrial a/c equipment.

	Factor A	Factor B	Factor C
Production Engineer (PE)	Energy Savings/ Protection Low Operating Cost Modernness	Modularity Noise Level	Complexity Field Tested
Top Manager (TM)	Energy Savings/ Protection Low Operating Cost Modernness Protection against Power Failure	Reliability/ Field Tested Initial Cost	Noise Level
HVAC Consultant (HC)	Energy Savings/ Protection Modernness	Reliability/ Field Tested	Noise Level Initial Cost

TABLE 7: COMPARISON OF FACTOR STRUCTURES FOR PE, TM AND HC

In sum, our analysis of the evaluation space for each group suggests that they not only differ in the number of evaluation criteria but, that substantial variation appears in the composition of those criteria. Different marketing strategies, including product positioning and salesmen presentations, can be targeted at these different groups to take advantage of these differences.

The next question is whether the evaluation analysis, performed at such a disaggregate level is behaviorally meaningful: does the consideration of these specific, and different evaluation criteria lead to a better understanding of the way decision participants form preferences?

The link between individuals' preferences for the three alternatives and their evaluation of these alternatives along the appropriate evaluation criteria

A1. The evaluation criteria are the same across decision participant groups as are preference parameters.

A2. The evaluation criteria are the same across groups but preference parameters differ.

A3: Both the evaluation criteria and the preference parameters differ across groups.

The two measures of preference requested in the questionnaire -- ranks and constant sum paired comparisons -- were used to eliminate individuals inconsistent in their preference judgements Although not statistically significant, our results indicate that corporate people (TM, CE) are less consistent in their preference judgements than people working at the plant level (PM, PE)

Two sets of regression were run. First, the actual rank-order was used as a dependent variable with the estimated factor scores as independent variables. Although our dependent variable is only ordinal, available empirical evidence suggests that least square regressions closely approximate monotonic regression for integer rank order preference variables (Green [10], Hauser and Urban [13]). Second, the constant sum paired comparison preference data were transformed to a ratio scale via Torgerson's [27] method, and used as a dependent variable.

Preference recoveries (for both first preferences and the actual rank order of each individual's preferences) are sensible goodness of fit measures for preference regressions and have been extensively reported in the literature (Hauser and Urban [13], Wildt and Bruno [3]). With three alternatives, a random model would recover first preference 1/3 of the time and give total preference recovery 1/6 of the time.

Table 8 summarizes the preference recovery results under all three sets

of evaluation criteria and preference parameters is considered (Assumption A3). An unexpected result is that the average preference recovery is somewhat superior under assumption A1 (that is homogeneous evaluation criteria and homogeneous preference parameters) than under assumption A2 (homogeneous evaluation criteria and heterogeneous preference parameters). This finding indicates that although A2 is a reasonable assumption in consumer marketing research (Allaire [1], Hauser [12]) it might not be reasonable in industrial markets, where different groups of decision participants exhibit substantial divergence in their perceptions of product alternatives and in their evaluation criteria.

	A1 Homogeneous Evaluation Criteria Homogeneous Preference Parameters	A2 Homogeneous Evaluation Criteria Heterogeneous Preference Parameters	A3 Heterogeneous Evaluation Criteria Heterogeneous Preference Parameters
1st Preference Recovery	67	.65	.72
All Preference Recovery	.44	.41	.52

TABLE 8: AVERAGE PREFERENCE RECOVERY

Table 9 gives the results for the rank-regression under assumption A3 for all five groups. Similar results were obtained by the use of ratio-scaled preferences and are reported by Choffray [4].

The results listed in Table 9 suggest interesting differences in the way product evaluations are related to individual preferences within each group. First, consider Corporate Engineers and Plant Managers (Table 6 interprets

cost most important while Plant Managers find modernness, fuel savings and low operating costs to be most significant

Group	Constant	Regression Coefficients 1st Factor	Regression Coefficients 2nd Factor	Regression Coefficients 3rd Factor	No. of Observations
CE	2.02	-.46	-.10	x	115
PM	2.00	-.25	-.19	x	84
PE	1.99	-.39	.27	(.09)*	66
TM	1.99	-.37	-.18	-.13	123
HC	1.99	(-.02)*	-.31	-.45	273

* not significantly different from 0 at the .10 level.

TABLE 9: RANK-PREFERENCE REGRESSION COEFFICIENTS UNDER A3

The comparison of the other three groups is most interesting. Production Engineers find modernness, low operating cost and protection against fuel rationing most important. But they seem to favor more complex, less noisy and potentially more risky alternatives (seen from the positive sign of that regression coefficient). Production Engineers are perhaps the only individuals in the decision process who will work with this equipment directly and, seem to favor that equipment which makes their job more challenging. Top managers also find modernness, protection and low operation cost most important, but weight reliability and initial cost heavily as well, in the expected direction. Finally, HVAC consultants do not seem concerned about modern image, low operating cost, and fuel rationing protection Their concerns are immediate -- they weight initial cost and noise level most heavily and, secondarily reliability and the presence of field proven components.

Hence, each of these groups not only evaluates the various alternatives differently, but the nature of the link between products evaluations and individual preferences is different as well. It is important to note that the preference regressions run under A2 -- common evaluation space and heterogeneous preference parameters (not reported here) -- suggested neither the positive association with system complexity noted above for Production Engineers (PE), nor the absence of association with modernness, low operating cost and fuel rationing protection for HVAC consultants (HC). The use of this new methodology is, then, a necessary step in the identification of these important psychological differences among decision groups.

7.0 Marketing Implications

The previous sections suggested important differences in the way various groups of decision participants perceive and evaluate industrial air conditioning systems. A well-integrated marketing and R&D program will tap these differences in both a product design and a marketing communications program.

Table 9 summarizes the differences between these groups.

	Issues of Key Importance	Issues of Less Importance
Production Engineer (PE)	modernness protection against fuel rationing complexity	first cost
Corporate Engineer (CE)	reliability first cost	modernness of image energy savings
Plant Manager (PM)	protection against fuel rationing modernness low operating cost	first cost
Top Manager (TM)	protection against fuel rationing modernness low operating cost	noise level in plant ease of component replacement
HVAC Consultant (HC)	noise level in plant first cost reliability	modernness low operating cost

TABLE 10· IMPORTANCE OF ISSUES TO DIFFERENT GROUPS OF DECISION PARTICIPANTS

The table suggests that, when communicating to Top managers and Plant Managers, low operating and initial costs must be stressed, along with modernness of company image and protection against fuel rationing. When promoting the new

Referring back to Table 3, it appears that HVAC consultants perceive LABS to be considerably less reliable than the other two systems. The eference analysis indicates this to be a key item affecting HVAC system eference. Thus, this information isolates areas in need of engineering provement and determines what messages a communication program might rget at a particular group.

The key contributions of the new methodology of importance to the intro ction of solar a/c (and to industrial marketers in general) fall under two tegories

A. Differences in Product Perception:

- Identification of characteristics of the new system which are not perceived by some group as management would like, so that corrective action can be taken.

- Development of advertising copy which accounts for the specific needs and requirements of each group of decision participants

B. Evaluation Criteria Differences

- Identification of areas of potential weaknesses in design and positioning by assessing the new product's position in the evaluation space relative to that of competitors.

- Development of salesmen's presentations and salesforce strategies that account for the specific needs of the different decision participants.

- Development of communication programs directed at particular groups of participants, making use of their specific sources of information.

8.0 Conclusions and Implications for Research

The key implications of this work for the marketing of new industrial products are that

- the way industrial products are perceived by different groups of decision participants differ substantially, and that
- the evaluation criteria, along which decision participants assess product alternatives, differ from one group to another.

An important result of this analysis is that differences in product perception and evaluation criteria among different groups involved in the adoption of a new industrial product must be explicitly included in an analysis of individual preferences.

Choffray and Lilien [5] have outlined how this information can be used in an industrial market response model. Their procedure first requires the identification of the target market for the new industrial product (called macrosegmentation). Organizations' selection criteria are then measured along with the structure of their adoption processes. This information is used to form microsegments of the potential market, in which companies exhibit a similar pattern of adoption process involvement Individual preferences are then investigated for each relevant group of decision participants, and individual choice models are calibrated. An estimate of the expected market share for the new product can then be obtained under various assumptions about the type of interaction occurring in each microsegment

The work reported in this paper is then part of a research plan aimed eveloping better tools for analyzing industrial markets. Here, we ssed the analysis of the process of perception evaluation and preference different actors in the industrial adoption process. This field of arch is in need of better models and measurement tools The results indicate that potential for improvement exists.

APPENDIX 1

USE OF THE CHOW TEST IN ESTABLISHING EQUALITY OF SEVERAL FACTORS OBTAINED FROM THE SAME SET OF VARIABLES IN DIFFERENT SAMPLES

A1. The Chow Test: Consider two regression models

(1) $Y_1 = X_1\beta_1 + \varepsilon_1$

(2) $Y_2 = X_2\beta_2 + \varepsilon_2$

where Y_i is $(n_i \times 1)$, X_i is $(n_i \times m)$, β_1 and β_2 are vectors of coefficients and ε_1, ε_2 are vectors of disturbances. The null hypothesis, $\beta_1 = \beta_2$ gives rise to the reduced model

(3) $Y = \begin{bmatrix} X_1 \\ X_2 \end{bmatrix} \beta + \varepsilon$

If we let e_1, e_2 and e be residual vectors associated with least squares estimation of (1), (2) and (3), respectively, then Chow [ ] shows that, under the null hypotheses,

(4) $C = \left\{ \frac{e'e}{e_1' e_1 + e_2' e_2} - 1 \right\} \frac{N-2m}{m}$

is distributed as F with m, (N-2m) d.f. (where $N = n_1 + n_2$).

A2. Application to the Comparison of Factors Obtained in Different Samples

The common factor analysis model expresses each observed variable $\{z_j, j=1,\ldots q\}$ as a linear combination of a small number of common factors

$\{F_p, p=1,\ldots m\}$ with $m \leq q$ plus a unique factor U_j

$$(5) \quad z_{ji} = \sum_{p=1}^{m} a_{jp} F_{pi} + k_j U_{ji} \quad ,$$

where a_{jp} and k_j are the factor pattern coefficients, and subscript i refers to a particular individual in the sample ($i=1,\ldots n$).

The factors F_p, $p=1,\ldots m$, however, are hypothetical unobserved constructs. In the case of most common factor analysis techniques, the factor scores have to be estimated indirectly. Linear regression on the original variables z_j, $j=1,\ldots q\}$ is often used for this purpose (Harman [11]). The model may be expressed as follows:

$$(4) \quad F_{pi} = \sum_{j=1}^{q} \beta_{pj} \cdot z_{ji} + \varepsilon_{pi}$$

where β_{pj} is the regression coefficient of factor F_p on variable z_j.

When the common factors are orthogonal, Harman [11] shows that R_p, the coefficient of multiple correlation associated with the estimation of factor F_p, can be calculated as

$$(5) \quad R^2_p = \sum_{j=1}^{q} b_{pj} \, s_{jp}$$

where the b_{pj}'s are least squares estimates of the β_{pj}'s and $\{s_{jp}, j=1,\ldots q, p=1\ldots m\}$, are the correlations between the original variable z_j's and the factor F_p's.

Under the usual assumptions of the common factor analysis model, it can be shown (Choffray [5]) that:

$$(6) \quad \sum_{i=1}^{n} (F_{pi} - \hat{F}_{pi})^2 = n(1-R_p^2)$$

We can then use (6) in (4), as $\sum_{i=1}^{n} (F_{pi} - \hat{F}_{pi})^2$ is the sum of the squared residuals $e'_p e_p$ associated with the estimation of the factor scores F_p.

Hence, the statistic

$$(7) \quad C_p = \left[\frac{N(1-R_p^2)}{n_1(1-R_{p1}^2) + n_2(1-R_{p2}^2)} - 1 \right] \frac{N-2q}{q}$$

can be used to test the equality of a specific factor obtained from the same set of variables in two different samples, where

R_{p1}^2, R_{p2}^2 are the squared multiple correlations associated with the estimation of factor p in sample 1 and 2 respectively,

R_p^2 is the squared multiple correlation associated with factor p in the pooled sample, and

N $= n_1 + n_2$

The test is readily extendable to the case where more than two samples are included in the analysis.

APPENDIX 2

ROTATED FACTOR LOADING MATRICES FOR THE FIVE GROUPS*

(*Note: See Table 1 for complete description of items.)

	FACTOR 1	FACTOR 2	FACTOR 3
Item 1	-0.22316	0.42747	-0.56334
Item 2	0.46540	-0.39623	0.07877
Item 3	-0.25144	0.66075	-0.58387
Item 4	0.65962	-0.26155	0.03730
Item 5	-0 02264	0.47154	-0.35798
Item 6	0 75290	-0.00082	0.30641
Item 7	0 76803	-0.02595	0.29846
Item 8	0 02738	0.60433	-0.04732
Item 9	0 35929	-0.32116	0.70671
Item 10	0.75243	-0.24124	0.26847
Item 11	-0.07375	-0.03003	0.62834
Item 12	0.76282	0.09390	-0.04418
Item 13	0.61089	-0.05849	-0.15229
Item 14	-0.10680	0.61909	-0.10051

Percentage of the common variance reproduced by the 3 factors: 87%

TABLE 12: VARIMAX ROTATED FACTOR MATRIX FOR TM

	FACTOR 1	FACTOR 2	FACTOR 3
Item 1	-0.09834	0.70547	0.07601
Item 2	0.61259	-0.29941	-0 19113
Item 3	-0 30730	0.77046	0.31167
Item 4	0.65816	-0.05916	-0.07040
Item 5	0 07488	0.55076	0.46701
Item 6	0.81028	-0.20987	-0.08010
Item 7	0.81101	-0.25434	-0.02270
Item 8	-0.13723	0.38997	0.18660
Item 9	0 26682	-0.74154	-0 20041
Item 10	0 70086	-0.31026	-0.11608
Item 11	-0 17011	-0.59742	0.10276
Item 12	0.71900	0.12102	0.04088
Item 13	0 54980	0.19404	0.06809
Item 14	-0 07618	0.20695	0 97375

Percentage of the common variance reproduced by the 3 factors: 90%

	Factor 1	Factor 2
Item 1	0.71613	-0.17387
Item 2	-0.35160	0.14687
Item 3	0.80057	-0.31993
Item 4	-0.15252	0.61189
Item 5	0.76775	0.01970
Item 6	-0 01547	0.76712
Item 7	-0.24906	0.80415
Item 8	0.40947	0.18330
Item 9	-0.81782	0.41061
Item 10	-0.32790	0.69898
Item 11	-0.48200	0.11139
Item 12	-0.06724	0.46189
Item 13	0.17781	0.44631
Item 14	0.55548	0.05201

Percentage of the common variance reproduced by the 2 factors. 83%

TABLE 14: VARIMAX ROTATED FACTOR MATRIX FOR PM

	Factor 1	Factor 2
Item 1	-0.06350	0.79864
Item 2	0.51733	-0 36001
Item 3	-0.34726	0.83285
Item 4	0.58111	0.05618
Item 5	-0.23362	0.38299
Item 6	0.78108	-0.25548
Item 7	0.67658	-0.25569
Item 8	0.07472	0 61947
Item 9	0.26725	-0.71792
Item 10	0.82866	-0.23721
Item 11	-0.18898	-0.44761
Item 12	0.74933	0 08457
Item 13	0.59198	-0.02587
Item 14	-0.34224	0.50309

TABLE 15. VARIMAX ROTATED FACTOR MATRIX FOR HC

	FACTOR 1	FACTOR 2	FACTOR 3
Item 1	-0.01453	0.77400	0.16627
Item 2	0.32379	-0.13874	-0 31433
Item 3	-0.16840	0.88049	0.20698
Item 4	0.76014	-0.16269	-0.25089
Item 5	-0.04686	0.53063	0.66995
Item 6	0.62641	-0.32135	-0.10489
Item 7	0.71850	-0.30453	-0.10532
Item 8	0.28045	0.27643	0.29778
Item 9	0 20946	-0.54396	-0.21152
Item 10	0.71165	-0.34161	-0.13029
Item 11	0 09245	-0.35529	-0.25870
Item 12	0 49252	0.17796	0.25933
Item 13	0.52640	0.23294	0.13880
Item 14	-0 03456	0.13695	0.59170

Percentage of the common variance reproduced by the three factors: 94%

REFERENCES

1. Allaire, Yvan. "The Measurement of Heterogeneous Semantic, Perceptual and Preference Structures," unpublished Ph.D. thesis, Massachusetts Institute of Technology, 1973.

2. Box, G E. P "A General Distribution Theory for a Class of Likelihood Criteria," Biometrika, 36, (1949), 317-346.

3. Cheston, Richard and Philip Doucet "Marketing Strategy Determination through Analysis of Purchasing Decision Structures in the HVAC Industry," unpublished Masters Thesis, Massachusetts Institute of Technology, 1976.

4. Choffray, Jean-Marie and Gary L. Lilien, "Models of the Multiperson Choice Process with Application to the Adoption of Industrial Products," Sloan School Working Paper No. 861-76, June 1976.

5. Choffray, Jean-Marie. "A Methodology for Investigating the Structure of the Industrial Adoption Process and the Differences in Perceptions and Evaluation Criteria among Potential Decision Participants," Forthcoming Ph.D. Thesis, Massachusetts Institute of Technology, 1977.

6. Chow, Gregory C. "Test of Equality Between Subsets of Coefficients in Two Linear Regressions," Econometrica, 38, (1960), 691-605.

7. Cooley, William W. and Paul R. Lohnes. Multivariate Data Analysis, (New York: John Wiley, 1971).

8. Daniels, Farrington, Direct Use of the Sun's Energy (New York. Ballantine Books, 1974).

9. Greenstreet, Richard L. and Robert J. Connor. "Power of Tests for Equality of Covariance Matrices," Technometrics, 16, (February 1974), 27-30.

10. Green, Paul E. "On the Robustness of Multidimensional Scaling Techniques," Journal of Marketing Research, 12 (February 1975), 73-81.

11 Harman, Harry H. Modern Factor Analysis (Chicago: The University of Chicago Press, 1976).

12 Hauser, John R "A Normative Methodology for Predicting Consumer Response to Design Decisions: Issues, Models, Theory and Use," unpublished Ph.D. Thesis, Massachusetts Institute of Technology, 1975.

13. Hauser, John R. and Glen L. Urban, "A Normative Methodology for Modeling Consumer Response to Innovation," Sloan School of Management Working Paper No 785-75.

15. Humphreys, L. G. and D. R. Ilgen. "Note on a Criterion for the Number of Common Factors," Educational and Psychological Measurement, 29, (1969), 571-578.

16. Lehmann, Donald R. and John O'Shaughnessy. "Difference in Attribute Importance for Different Industrial Products," Journal of Marketing, Volume 38, No. 2 (April 1974), 36-42.

17. Lilien, Gary L. "A Socio-Economic and Marketing Study for a Standard Fomento Factory In Puerto Rico -- Year 1 Report." Dialogue, Inc. Report, (September 1976).

18. Lilien, Gary L. and Paul E. Johnston, "A Study of the Potential for and Impact of a Solar Water Heating Industry in New England," Dialogue, Inc. Report (July 1976).

19. Little, Arthur D. Inc., Solar Heating and Cooling Constraints and Incentives: A Review of the Literature, March 1976.

20 Miller, G. A. "The Magical Number Seven, Plus or Minus Two: Some Limits on our Capacity for Processing Information," Psychological Review, 63 (1956), 81-97.

21 Montanelli, Richard G., Jr., and Lloyd G. Humphreys. "Latent Roots of Random Data Correlation Matrices with Squared Multiple Correlations on the Diagonal: A Monte Carlo Study," Psychometrika, 41, (September 1976), 341-348.

22. Morrison, Donald F. Multivariate Statistical Methods, 2nd ed. (New York: McGraw-Hill, 1976).

23. New England Electric System. Solar Energy, Today and Tommorow, (October 1975)

24. Rogers, Everett M. and F. Floyd Shoemaker, Communication of Innovations, 2nd edition (New York. The Free Press, 1971).

25. Scott, Jerome E. and Peter Wright. "Modeling an Organizational Buyer's Product Evaluation Strategy: Validity and Procedural Considerations," Journal of Marketing Research, 13 (August 1976), 211-224.

26 Sheth, Jagdish N. "A Model of Industrial Buyer Behavior," Journal of Marketing, 37, (October 1973), 50-56.

27 Torgerson, Warren S. Theory and Methods of Scaling (New York: John Wiley and Sons, 1958).

28. Tybout, R. A. and G.O.G. Löf. "Solar House Heating," Natural Resources Journal, Vol. 10, No. 2 (April 1970).

30. Webster, Frederick E. Jr and Yoram Wind. Organizational Buying Behavior (Englewood Cliffs,N.J.: Prentice-Hall, 1972).

31. Westinghouse Electric Corporation, Solar Heating and Cooling of Buildings. Phase 0 (May 1974).

32. Wildt, Albert R. and Albert U. Bruno. "The Prediction of Preference for Capital Equipment Using Linear Attitude Models," Journal of Marketing Research, 11 (May 1974), 203-205.

33. Williams, J. Richard Solar Energy: Technology and Applications (Ann Arbor, MI: Ann Arbor Science Publishers, 1974).

www.ingramcontent.com/pod-product-compliance
Lightning Source LLC
LaVergne TN
LVHW020034170826
845678LV00001B/244
* 9 7 8 0 3 5 3 2 4 0 4 4 5 *